Child Heart

Notes from a Kindergarten Teacher

Janice Strootman

Cloud 9 Publishing
Cloud9publ.wordpress.com

ISBN 978-1-886352-44-5

Cover photo by Christine Fragio.

Author's contact:
Email: jstrootman@gmail.com

Acknowledgments:

Thanks to all from whom I have solicited advice over the past two years while writing this book. Thank you to my publisher, Nadia Giordana, to Gretchen Marquette, and my poetry cohort Lee Colin Thomas, Kathleen Kimball Baker, and Kelly Westoff, and to my editors, Mary Nosek, Marge Barrett, Kate Petit, Susan P. McCarthy, Maria Marcucci, and Ann Sturdivant. Thank you also, to my WOW 1 group for teaching me so much! I am grateful to all of you and to those I may have missed.

I want to say a special thank you to my daughter Sarah, my son Paul, and their families.

Thank you most of all to my husband, Denny, who has supported me every step of the way.

Finally, this book would not be possible without the many students whose curiosity, precocity, and spirit inspired my teaching and accompanied me on my journey as an educator.

PROLOGUE

When I Started…

Blonde curls bounced around my head as I raced into the front yard, heading straight for the pothole in our driveway. It had filled with water in the thunderstorm the night before. My bare feet trod over the ridges in the dirt, packed tightly from the pummeling rain. I plopped myself down in the puddle and felt mud and water flow around my bare legs and sapphire blue bathing suit. My hands grabbed the squishy mud. I watched it slowly ooze through my fingers and down to my elbows, leaving streaks like roads all along my arms. These were my childhood roads. As I grew, so did my pathways—ultimately leading me to seven continents, fifty countries, and fifty states.

Growing up with no neighbors within walking distance, I played by myself a lot in the dense woods surrounding our house and swam in a small lake close by. I always loved nature–water, trees, and my dad's big vegetable garden, in particular.

Munching on carrots
pulled fresh from the rich black soil,
just lightly brushed off.

Janice Strootman

I would sit in the dirt in front of the cabbage plants that were lined up in two rows. I saw all the plants at once, unlike all the rows of corn that seemed to go on forever in the farmer's fields. I tapped a small oak branch on my knee and talked to the cabbages as if they were my students.

"Your leaves are a little brown. Maybe you need some water?" To the next one, I said, "You are smaller than the others. Do we need to put more manure around you?" Another one had insect bites around one of its leaves. "The bugs are getting to you, but you are pretty big. Time for you to get picked!" I steadily went down the row, analyzing each one, suggesting what needed to be done to get the best result.

Dad sat on the wooden bench, drinking the cold glass of water I'd brought him and watched me. After dinner, I heard him tell my mom, "Janice is going to be a teacher someday. She's out in the garden teaching the vegetables!"

And so I was and so I did.

Janice Strootman

TABLE OF CONTENTS

Janice Strootman

Introduction

A quote I like is, "Only those who look with the eyes of children can lose themselves in the object of their wonder." by Eberhard Arnold. I have tried to see the world in that light. You can be an inspired teacher if you love learning. There is an art to teaching that you either have or you don't. You need to see, hear, feel, and touch, a child's heart.

Most of my career, I taught kindergarten. I also taught every age of pupil from preschool to adulthood. I got to live in many beautiful locations around the world.

The first selection in the book, *Teaching at Spring Lake,* documents the first inklings of my journey. As a child, I had no idea what my life would bring, but there were clues that I would become a teacher and have opportunities to travel the world.

I grew up in Mounds View, a first-tier suburb of Minneapolis/St. Paul. I attended the University of Minnesota, graduated from Winona State University with a degree in education and an additional certificate for kindergarten. While at the University, I met my husband Denny. He also became a teacher, and we shared our lives together.

I started out as a kindergarten teacher in the Roseville School District just north of St. Paul, Minnesota, in 1971. I was young and enthusiastic. I realized early on that teaching was a good fit for me, because I wanted to be a life-long learner. Some of the anecdotes in Section 1 chronicle my earliest experiences from chasing frogs around the classroom to giving mouth-to-beak resuscitation to a duck. I learned very quickly how these little five-year-olds were all individuals navigating the world as they perceived and understood it. They gave me a chance to see it through their eyes.

My job assignments changed while in the Roseville District, and they changed a lot. While still a young teacher, I earned my master's degree from Mankato State University in Early Childhood. One of my jobs outside of the classroom was planning topics for discussions with parents of four-year-old children. During one period, I worked in administration as districtwide volunteer coordinator, and director of public relations. Ultimately, I returned to my first love, the classroom.

Parkview Center School turned from a junior high to an alternative elementary school in 1989. It is there that I developed a lot of the lessons, units, and programs that proved successful for my students over the years.

At the end of Section 1, *Starry Night* and *Five Major Religions* relate to that time. The real joy of teaching was the relationship I established with students. To this day, I am in contact with many, both here and abroad.

During the time I worked in Roseville, Denny and I had our two children, Sarah and Paul. We were living the American dream: A house, two cars, two kids, and good steady jobs. Plus, like many Minnesotans, we had a lake cabin.

The biggest change occurred in 2000 when both kids were off to college. We were recruited by a former Roseville principal to work at Hong Kong International School. Initially we were undecided, but with the encouragement of our kids, we pulled up stakes and moved to Hong Kong. Section II of the book highlights some of my experiences there.

Hong Kong is a magnificent place to work and live. It is visually stunning, located on the south coast of China, on the South China Sea. It was a "world away" from our experience in mid-western U.S.—physically and culturally. Aside from that, it was incredibly easy to adapt to our new home. We quickly learned to navigate a city of seven million people using mass transit. *Out and About in Hong Kong* relates one of my more infamous trips on a local bus.

I learned a lot about expat culture in Hong Kong. Parents and staff had high expectations of their teachers. During the first year, I taught grade one, but I was able to transfer to kindergarten after that. Denny and I lived on the fifteenth floor of a high-rise attached to my school, and I took the elevator to work. Talk about an easy commute! Many of the programs I helped develop in Minnesota were adapted for use in Hong Kong as part of the curriculum at the lower primary. We had families from all over the world—forty-one different countries. Students were required to speak English in school.

Hong Kong was very international. We loved learning everything we could about it and experiencing its culture first hand. The expat community was also extensive—a mix of Americans, Australians, Brits, Canadians, Europeans, Africans, and South Asians. We experienced so much more than Chinese culture. We also learned about the division between rich and poor. Most Hong Kong citizens work to just "get by." But there was also an international crowd of ultra-wealthy who occupied the exclusive high rises along the ridges above the city. They anchored gigantic yachts in the city's harbors, and had homes in numerous countries. Many of their children attended Hong Kong International. Stories in Section II, such as *We're not in Kansas*

Anymore, and *Dripping with Diamonds* highlight our experiences with the very wealthy.

Our nine years in Hong Kong were wonderful, but a little more complicated than I've let on. September 11 occurred while we were there as recounted in *Different but the Same.* The SARS epidemic also took place. I contracted a serious lung infection (not SARS) that necessitated my return to Minnesota. Denny continued teaching in Hong Kong. We worked separately for two years, but reunited in Hong Kong after I retired.

When Denny retired in 2009, we packed up and moved back to Minnesota. Since we had previously sold our house in Roseville, we purchased a little condo in Bloomington, Minnesota, close to the airport and the Mall of America. We still had the lake cabin.

Our kids were both married and lived in different parts of the world. Our daughter married a Naval officer, so she and her family lived in Japan, California, and Hawaii. Our son married a girl he met in San Diego. They both went into international teaching. Their first assignment was in Venezuela, and the second in Brazil. At the time of this writing, they are in Dubai.

In looking back, I was not only astonished by the opportunity of teaching in Hong Kong, but by the opportunity to travel to many locations in Asia. We went to Australia and New Zealand, but hadn't spent a lot of time in Europe. Both Denny and I were in good health and felt we could take on a new school if it meant a chance to live and work there. We met a couple at our Bloomington condo who became good friends. They had worked for a company called QSI (Quality Schools International). They encouraged us to apply, and we were offered and accepted a position in Minsk, Belarus in 2014. There's a lot of history in Minsk. It was literally blown off the map in WWII! It was rebuilt and turned into a new, family-friendly city.

Denny taught secondary language arts, and social studies. My teaching position was for pre-kindergarten and I had sixteen students, only two of whom spoke English. I resorted to teaching via pantomime and sign language. Charlie Chaplin had nothing on me! I had a lovely, young assistant named Olga who spoke English and Belorussian in case we needed an interpreter. Another cheerful aide, Ksenia, helped supervise lunch and recess.

The school where we taught was located in an old house in a residential area. Our apartment was immense by local standards, and more than adequate for our needs. Again we used mass transit to get around. We thoroughly enjoyed the culture, taking in some ballet, and concerts. The staff at the school was friendly and helpful.

Much of Section 3 of the book contains stories from my time in Minsk.

Denny and I returned to Minnesota, but with the idea that we could possibly be coaxed back to Europe if another opportunity arose. And one did!

This time it came from our next-door neighbors at our lake cabin. They had joined a program sponsored by the Evangelical Lutheran Church of America to teach in Bratislava, Slovakia. They loved it and encouraged us to apply, so, we did. We were expecting a position in Bratislava, the biggest city and capital of Slovakia, but instead were offered volunteer positions as English lectors in Liptovsky Mikulas, in the north-central part of the country, right in the Tatra Mountains. It was a lovely village with a quaint plaza in the middle of town next to a large reservoir. Slovakia is the hidden gem of Europe—it's beautiful and the people are so gracious.

For me, it was the first time teaching in a high school. I was nervous about the prospect of teaching older, almost adult, students. I also taught two classes of sixth-graders at the primary school.

As English lectors, our purpose was to get the students to speak. I had to adapt my methods so I could use my elementary background, but the students seemed to love it. Again, we found everything about our situation exciting. I did discover, however, when working with older students, the problems they face are bigger and more serious, so there was that side of it as well. The pieces in Section 3 are from our time in Slovakia.

After returning to our home in Minnesota and selling our cabin, I set about writing the stories I've included in this book. I have written a lot of poetry, some of which has been published in literary magazines. This book consists of haibun, short prose ending with a haiku.

I have tried to capture the essence of my teaching life, both through my eyes and from the heart of a child. All the stories I have written focus on the ups and downs, ins and outs of teaching. I enjoyed attending workshops to improve my teaching and learn new skills. I saw it as a challenge to discover how well I could understand and teach skills important for students to learn.

When I played Sister Jan (a teaching nun) in a show called, *The Great Kindergarten Pajama Jam,* the words written by Hillevi Peterson-Hirsch summed it up, "You came into the classroom such a long, long way from home, feelin' kind of nervous, feelin' all alone. Let me introduce myself. I am your new best friend. We can help each other learn, on that you can depend. Because I teach. Oh yes, I teach."

I hope you enjoy this book. Thank you for reading.

Janice Strootman

Section 1

Minnesota

Teaching at Spring Lake

I was fifteen years old when my teaching career began. I served as an apprentice swimming instructor and taught lessons to young children at a beach near my home. I felt so grown up because I was offered $.75 an hour. I taught five to seven-year-olds every forty-five minutes until noon, Monday through Friday, for eight weeks every summer until I was eighteen.

I wore a red, two-piece bathing suit that covered my navel. A whistle hung around my neck on a red lanyard, and zinc oxide slathered my face, shoulders, and the tops of my bare feet. I wore a baseball cap over long, blonde, wavy hair. The kids were cute in their small bathing suits with their round tummies. They were excited and apprehensive at the same time. I was too!

I really didn't know what I was doing, but I watched a more experienced teacher next to me and followed what she did. When her students laid on their bellies and did the flutter kick along the shoreline, my students did too. When her students gathered in a circle around her and practiced rhythmic breathing, so did mine. I carried a clipboard with the names of my students and checked each one as they ran towards me when their parents dropped them off in the parking lot. Some parents dashed off to run errands and others flipped down a towel to sit and watch.

I loved talking to the parents, and the fifteen minutes between classes never felt like enough time for that. I was thrilled to teach children by myself and wanted to learn everything about them. They were capable, uninhibited, and open to learning anything and everything. I learned quickly how to manage my time.

Scent of fish and weeds
snails and foamy white water
bring me to Spring Lake.

I Guess it Was for Me

At twenty-one, I fit the stereotype of the syrupy-sweet kindergarten teacher. I spoke softly in a high, gushy voice, exuded positive energy, and was dramatic in word and action. I had a pixie haircut, wore dangly earrings and short skirts, and walked jauntily down the hallways.

My first year of teaching, I had twenty-eight students. On the fourth day of class, my twenty-ninth student arrived. The day was just starting when in walked our neighborhood foster mother with one of her charges in tow–a child who had been removed from his home because his parents had taught him to set fires so they could claim insurance money. Michael had freshly Brylcreemed hair, and a major scowl on his face. His hands gripped tight the six-shooters buckled low around his hips, his cowboy-booted feet planted far apart. His harried foster mom had an apple in her hand. She handed it to him and gave him a nudge. I bent down eye-level with him and said in a sugary voice, "Oh, Michael, is that for me?" He stood silent, glaring for a moment and then said, "Who in the hell do you think it's for?"

Janice Strootman

Don't ask a question
to which you know the answer–
it's embarrassing!

Readin' and Writin'

Having a child who could read at a young age was a point of pride for parents, but I felt applying too much pressure was the quickest way for a child's self-esteem to nosedive. I tried to make it fun for them instead.

Our class had a hound-dog puppet, Bowser, who lived on top of the piano in our room, and he brought his alphabet friends to class every Monday. I gave him a deep voice and had him tell stories–*Andy the Astronaut* through *Zelda Zebra.* Students would take copies of the stories, find the designated letters, count them, print the number at the top of the paper, print their name, and color a picture of each of the alphabet friends. These would go home so parents could reinforce the concepts of learning the name of the letter, sound, and words that began with it. We learned the digraphs *sh, ch, th, wh*, too. At the end of January, when we had finished all the letter puppets, we started putting the sounds together to make words.

During their play time, I worked individually with beginning reading students. They would sound out words in "easy" books I borrowed from textbooks published in the 1950's. I made ten copies of each reader so I had enough for the students to take home and practice with their parents.

I wish I had a nickel for every time I listened to *Nat is a cat. Nat is a fat cat! Is Nat fat? Nat is fat! Nat is a fat cat!* By the end of kindergarten, all my typical learners were able to read. It wasn't accomplished by pushing them but instead by making learning interesting through Bowser, alphabet friends, and journals. It involved both technique and art.

It was rewarding for me to see the expression on a child's face when she realized she was reading. It was a moment I knew she would never forget. I had enabled her to learn a lifelong skill. How does teaching get better than that?

Oh, what a process.
Learning to read can be hard.
It is my passion.

Initiation

As a first-year teacher, I could plan for some classroom events and others I could not. One day, during rest time, I was recording data in my plan book when I looked up and saw two boys self-pleasuring on their rugs. I thought my eyes were deceiving me. I sat there, not knowing what to do. A few more students tuned in and started doing the same thing. I went to put down my plan book, and saw a boy and girl under my desk, French kissing. Had the phases of the moon gone crazy? Had aliens landed and taken control of my class? I was stunned. I had never seen anything like it before, and it wasn't addressed in my teacher-preparatory classes.

I went over to the piano and started playing. This signaled the end of rest time and they knew to come and sit around the piano for music time. Students quietly got up, folded their rugs and put them away. As I looked down at their innocent, flushed little faces, I realized the song I had been playing was *When the Saints Go Marching In.*

I stuffed the memory of this situation deep down

until years later, when a junior-high-age young lady walked into my classroom and said, "Hi, do you remember me? You were my kindergarten teacher." She had changed quite a bit, but I still recognized her. She had the same chubby face. Before I could say anything, she went over to my desk, and looked under it. "Remember the day Greg and I were under here French kissing? I'm surprised we both fit!" My mouth dropped—I had successfully blocked the memory out. I looked at her and we both started laughing uncontrollably. It was funny ten years later, but not so much back then.

New experience!
How do you prepare for this?
Getting broken in—

Hopping Around the Hallways

Life science was one of my favorite subjects to teach kindergartners. In January, I received frog eggs from a science supply store and gave each child ten eggs in a 5"x9" clear plastic container. They were responsible for checking the water level and temperature each day and drawing the appearance of their eggs in their journals. We were fortunate to have a tree-lined creek running behind the playground–a great place to release the tadpoles when they became frogs in the spring.

We followed the life cycle from beginning to end. The eggs hatched into wiggly tadpoles. We fed them fish food so they would grow strong and healthy. When they got their back legs, the kids and I went out to the playground to find stones to put in the plastic containers so the tadpoles had something to jump on if their gills turned into lungs before we got back from our spring break, which was starting the next week. The tadpoles began getting their front legs the last day before vacation.

I was the first teacher to arrive back at school after spring break. The custodian was waiting for me at the door. He had his hands on his hips and a bandana over his nose. A smell like rotten cabbage hit me as I walked inside. Ninety percent of the tadpoles were frogs, their dead, slimy bodies plastered around the school hallways. The custodian handed me a bucket and a mop without saying a word. I spent the next two hours cleaning and disinfecting the floors and counters before my colleagues arrived. Lesson learned!

Life cycle of frogs.
Hopping around the hallways,
freedom was short-lived.

Dental Assistant

I pulled a thousand loose teeth during my career—something I wouldn't be allowed to do if teaching today. But my students were distracted when they had a loose tooth. They wiggled it, showed their friends, pulled at it, wiggled it some more, showed all the adults who came into class, and wiggled it a little more.

I took matters into my own hands and told my classes I was the best tooth-puller in the whole wide world and that when I "helped" a tooth come out, it never hurt! I put this information in the weekly newsletter and said if parents had any objections, they should let me know. I wasn't the best in the whole wide world for one student. His tooth had the longest root I had ever seen and it bled for twenty minutes! I ate humble pie when I called that parent to explain.

I checked a loose tooth daily. After a while, I could estimate how long it would be before I could pull it. When it was ready, the class gathered around, and my student stood next to me. I took a white envelope from my desk and wrote on the front: "To the Tooth Fairy, love from ____" and the child printed her name. I made eyes out of the "o's" in the word 'tooth' and asked whether she wanted the eyes to look up, sideways or down. This distracted her from the pending extraction. I took a tissue to "check" it and "plink!" out it popped! I was very matter of fact about the process so the children accepted it. I sealed the envelope with a noisy slurp, we laughed and got back to work.

This practice continued for many years, and as children advanced from class to class, they came to me to pull their teeth. I loved it because I could find out how they were and what was happening in their lives.

Baby teeth were fine.
I drew the line at molars.
They were pretty gross!

Older than Dirt

On orientation day for kindergartners, my colleague and I were on the sidewalk waiting for the children to arrive. One student rushed up to me and turned over my name tag, which had flipped over on my lanyard. "Hi, Miss Jan! My name is Greg. How old are you?"

I replied, "Older than dirt!" He ran his hands over the front of my dress and said, "Seriously, Miss Jan, how old are you?" I looked at him and remembered attending a meeting about this little guy the previous spring. I said, "Well, I was born in 1948." Without missing a beat, he replied, "Oh, you're forty-seven then." I said that sounded right.

He then asked me what kind of car I drove. "A Saturn," I said. "What color?" he asked. "Umm, it's a color between silver and brown, called taupe," I said. "I know what taupe is, silly!" he said. Before I could respond, he asked, "Is your license plate number KCC 433? BTP 949? *RCD 703?*" He then listed five other license plate numbers. I recognized mine and told him. Greg had memorized all these license plate numbers as his mother had driven through the parking lot looking for a space to park. I knelt down and said, "I think we are going to have a very interesting year! I am going to learn a lot!" He replied, "Good! I will help you all I can!"

I definitely felt "older than dirt" by June 10.

Please give me the strength
to teach this clever young man—
Serenity Prayer.

I Don't Think So Either, Ricky

When I taught about the circulatory system, I used a plastic see-through model of a human torso. It was fascinating to my five-year-olds to watch the mix of red food coloring and water run through the arteries and veins. I told them that under our skin, we looked just like the model.

We had a lot of hunters in Minnesota, and at my request, parent volunteers donated deer hearts to our classroom after the hunting season opened in November. With students gathered around me, I dissected a deer's heart using a scalpel, scissors, and pick. During choice time when children could choose their own activities, some students came over to the table and touched the heart, running their fingers through the vessels and asking questions. Ricky spent a half hour running his fingers through the heart and over the pieces I'd cut off with the scalpel. His mouth was open with his tongue curled, totally engrossed in his work. After a while, he looked up at me and said, "Miss Jan, I don't think this deer is going to live."

Janice Strootman

Woe to the deer heart
used to teach circulation.
Ricky still had hope.

Three States of Water

My students loved to eat snow on the playground during outside time in the winter.

I told them snow had dirt in it but some were skeptical about it. I decided to teach a lesson about the three states of water.

On the day we did this, it had snowed the previous evening, leaving the ground dazzling and pristine. My students scooped up fistfuls of it and plunked it into an empty ice cream bucket I carried.

We returned inside and transferred the snow (solid) into a clean saucepan. We put it on a hotplate and watched as it turned into water (liquid). Pretty soon it started to give off steam (water vapor), a gas. The children excitedly told me that there was no dirt! I said, "Just wait."

We put a white coffee filter on top of a quart canning jar and poured the remaining liquid through the filter. My students gasped and their eyes were alien-sized saucers! There, on the bottom of the filter were grains of dirt!

Janice Strootman

The next day, during our morning meeting, one of my students said, "I told my dad about the three states of water and he told me to tell you there are four states of water. I looked at him and said, "Really?" He proceeded to tell me that the stages of water are solid, liquid, gas, and plasma. I looked it up later and he was right. Just when I think I know what I'm talking about…

Plasma! What? Really?
Upstaged by a five-year-old
and his smart father!

I'm Glad I Studied

The children focused their attention on the globe and flashlight in front of me. The overhead lights were out. I demonstrated Earth's rotation, revolution, spring and autumnal equinox by shining the light on the globe. One student watched and listened to what I was saying. He had a puzzled expression on his face but sat totally still. When I was done with the presentation, I asked if anyone had questions or comments. Cliff raised his hand and said, "You know, Miss Jan, you did a pretty good job of explaining that!" His dad was a physics professor at the University of Minnesota.

Is it inspiring?
Children can learn anything
taught at their level.

Yodi

Back when pets were allowed in school, I brought Yodi, our rescue terrier poodle mix, to visit. We named Yodi after Yoda, the character in *Star Wars*, because of her large ears and squashed nose.

The kids loved her, and she loved them. Yodi had attached herself to me, the alpha female in our family. She followed me everywhere.

When I brought her to school, she walked down the hall with us like she was part of the school community—and she came to be. Students and staff doted on her, and the school secretaries and custodians gave her treats. She was even in our class picture that year.

Yodi was special.
She looked forward to coming
to our class each day.

Yodi could sense when someone was having a bad day and would go over to them, lie down, and rest her head at their feet. She provided emotional support for several students who endured difficult living situations at home. My kindergartners were not rowdy in her presence–they petted her and snuggled her. Having her in class that year was very calming.

She had huge brown eyes
that looked straight into your heart,
a gift of brown fur.

The Plan

"It's OK to make a mistake"

My class and I were lined up outside the library waiting to enter. Our school principal walked up beside me just as Hannah turned around with her hands on her hips and said to Ricky, "You are pushing me. I am angry. I want you to stop it." Hannah had just demonstrated *The Plan*.

My principal looked at me in amazement and said, "Did she just use *The Plan?"* I nodded and she continued, "Wow, that's great. I need to get that on the agenda for our next staff meeting. If kindergartners can do it, all of our students can."

The Plan is a three-step conflict-resolution method that evolved from the work of William Glasser and Diane Gossen on choice theory, reality therapy and restitution. My teaching partner and I attended workshops about the ideas of these educators and figured out a way to use them with young children.

We started by asking our kindergartners how we

could all feel safe in our classroom. We charted their responses and said, "It sounds like these ideas will keep us safe. These are called beliefs—things we want to happen all the time in class." We fine-tuned our beliefs and posted them in several places around the classroom.

We did an activity where the kids chose a partner, faced each other and slowly walked towards each other. They stopped when they felt uncomfortable. The area around them was called their personal space bubble. No one was allowed to enter it. If they did, we moved to the next step called *The Plan.*

The Plan
Step 1: Tell what happened.
We told the children to—Make yourself look big, look the offender in the eye and say "You…"

Step 2: Tell how you feel.
"I feel…"

Step 3: Tell what you need.
"I want you to…"

The students and I acted out scenarios where they hadn't felt safe until they knew the three steps by heart.

My colleague and I were pleased with how well it worked! We loved that it took "tattling" out of the conversation. Playground attendants mentioned they liked it for the same reason. The kids weren't coming up to them telling on their friends.

When Susan came to us and said "Kyle took my book," we asked, "Did you use *The Plan* with him?" If she hadn't, we watched while she did.

If Kyle ignored her or walked away, we reminded him that his "job" was to listen or the two of them would go through the restitution process. This involved each person talking about:

1.) What happened?
2.) Why was it important (offender) to do that? Could the action have been worse?
3.) How will you remedy the situation? What kind of friend/classmate do you want to be?

My colleague, teaching assistants, and I served as "guides by the side" to facilitate the process.

We were asked to make a video of *The Plan* for Diane Gossen and we also presented at the Minnesota Education Association fall conference.

How can you solve issues?
Children can handle problems
when given the tools.

Teaching Art and Craft

Art is freedom. "Creating" means children taking a deep breath and letting it go.

I differentiated between art projects and craft projects. A craft project was learning a new skill like paper-weaving, cutting snowflakes, tying string, or sewing a basic stitch. Once students learned a craft, they made projects using that skill in their own way. The product was individual and imaginative.

Kids are creative.
They have no preconceptions
of how art should look.

We discussed Judaism as part of a unit called *Celebrations Around the World.* Kids learned they could use their craft skills to make art. We made menorahs using every art material we could think of. These included paper-towel tubes, macaroni noodles, buttons, tongue depressors, straws, pipe cleaners, clay, tape, glue, crayons, markers, tissue paper, construction paper, stubby pencils and crayons, paper grocery bags, nails, wire, screws, screwdrivers, tin foil, crepe paper, string, toothpicks, tacks, cardboard, egg cartons, and more.

I sat my students in the middle of the circle of materials and talked about what we needed in order to make a menorah (a base, seven candles, one Shammash candle, flames). The children walked silently around the circle to look at the materials and formulate their ideas for making their own menorahs. They returned to their places on the floor and, when ready, quietly got up, chose materials, and found a quiet place to work. This project lasted about an hour and a half.

Each child's personality and learning style was evident in his or her menorah. They were diligent and proud of their finished products.

Some were neat and trim,
more streamed puddles of white glue.
Personality.

Starry Night

Vincent Van Gogh's *The Starry Night* was a piece my students imitated. They finger-painted 18" x 24" paper with purple and blue finger-paint, making swirls with their fingertips for the sky. They used the palms of their hands to make the horizon line between sky and land. They made yellow triangle stars, and cut construction paper squares, triangles, and rectangles for the village, and green paper curled with a scissors for the olive tree. The children loved learning about the masters.

After they learned about shape, texture, and design, I took my students to downtown Minneapolis, where they saw these concepts in the buildings and walkways. The kids noticed how shapes fitted together to make all kinds of interesting buildings. Some buildings couldn't be seen in their entirety because parts of others were in front of them. Perspective was a new and interesting concept to them.

On our field trip, we walked through part of the city, passing an art store. One of my students pointed to a Van Gogh print and said, "Look, there's 'The Starry Night' by Van Gogh. Cool." Two businessmen carrying briefcases and dressed in suits stopped and looked at him. "Did you hear that?" one of them said to the other. "Where do these kids pick up this stuff?" I walked on with a smile on my face as wide as the sky.

Back at school the next day, with classical music as their backdrop, they drew the city using black permanent markers and watercolor paints. Children sprawled all over the classroom and intently got to work. Each art piece was incredible in detail and personality. The results were frame worthy.

We can all create.
Art frees feelings inside us.
So necessary!

Playing Politics

I enjoyed having parent volunteers in my classroom. After spending a few hours in kindergarten, many would ask me, "How do you do this day after day?" Parents were my biggest advocates.

Oftentimes, parents stopped into the principal's office on their way out of the building to talk about unruly students and ask what could be done about them. Volunteers saw how I stopped class to deal with situations and asked how they could help me. I casually mentioned that I was doing all I could but that extra help was valuable.

One year, a student continually touched, teased, and sat too close to another child. He tried to kiss her, take her things and hide them in his backpack. The little girl's mother came in to volunteer, saw these behaviors and marched down to the office and in no uncertain terms, pressed the principal to remedy the situation. Within one week, there was a classroom assistant assigned to be with the offending child. I had previously discussed the situation in our weekly team meeting with the school psychologist, speech therapist, social worker, physical therapist and principal, but often the "process" took much longer to produce results than an angry parent. More often than not, I received the extra help I needed. Parents can be strong allies when given the opportunity. They were invaluable to me.

Had I played politics in this situation? Perhaps. The parent was not one who offered to volunteer in the classroom, but I called her and asked her if she would come into class for a "special" project. The scenario unfolded as I expected and the situation was rectified.

These situations take place daily. Classroom teachers need more help in managing challenging students. Educators see increasing numbers of pupils who have needs beyond what can be dealt with by a teacher alone in a classroom.

We work together,
parents, students and all staff,
to form the best team.

Ducks Limited

Every spring, the kids and I hatched chicken or duck eggs. After our chicks or ducklings were partly grown, we gave them to a local farmer. I went into school on weekends to sweep, change the bedding on the floor of the pen, refill water and food troughs, and make sure the warming lights were operating properly.

The first year we hatched ducklings, I had no prior experience. I read the teaching manual, talked to people who had done it before, and hoped for the best. The most difficult part was keeping the children from opening the incubator lid. If that happened, the eggs would not hatch.

Our first year progressed well. The ducklings hatched, and we watched as they waddled around their pen, drank water, ate grain, and grew feathers. There were three, so we named them Huey, Dewey, and Louie, after Donald Duck's three nephews.

One Saturday morning, I went into school to clean the pen. I couldn't let the ducklings have the run of the classroom, so I put them in a Rubbermaid plastic tub in the sink. I ran water to half-fill the tub and the ducklings quacked noisily, happy to be swimming around. I turned my back and began sweeping the poop-infused wood shavings from the floor. I worked for a few minutes and then noticed that the ducklings weren't quacking anymore. I raced over to the sink and all three ducklings were limp and I saw they weren't breathing. "Oh no!"

I had no idea what to do. I grabbed the first duckling and started mouth-to-beak resuscitation. I didn't know how hard to blow or for how long. I just did it, while massaging the little duckling's heart. Was it in the same place as ours?

After three little breaths, it opened its eyes and started breathing! I put it back in the water and it immediately started to flounder. I realized I had put too much water in the tub and the ducklings had gotten worn out paddling because they couldn't touch the bottom. I quickly dumped out some water and put the duckling back. He seemed OK so I grabbed the second duckling and gave it mouth-to-beak resuscitation. It took longer but that duckling finally came around, too. Unfortunately, the third one had been unresponsive for too long. I felt awful.

I took the dead duckling, put it in a garbage bag, and set it by the door. The two remaining ducklings started quacking again. I put them under the lights to help them dry off a little. I sat down in my chair and tried to stop shaking. Had I really put my mouth over a duckling's beak, twice? I sat there and thought about how to explain this to my students.

I thought of telling them that Huey decided to visit his aunt who lived down the street, or that he went to live with his grandma in Bemidji, or that he had turned into Super Duck and flew over to McCarron's Lake, but I ended up telling them the truth.

I put the dead duckling in the staff freezer next to my room and made it a point to get to school first on Monday to take it out. I didn't think my colleagues would enjoy knowing their lunch entree was keeping company with Huey. I took him out and showed the class what he looked like dead and put him back in the bag. We took him outside and I dug a hole and buried him in the school courtyard. They made a headstone for him out of paper towel tubes. When it started to disintegrate, I told them that the headstone and duckling were making grass for new plants to grow.

Trial and error failed.
Life science is sometimes not
ducks unlimited.

Five Major Religions and Cultural Holidays

Teaching social studies in the '80s and '90s revolved around whether schools could have a Christmas tree or sing Christmas songs. Our school board passed a regulation stating the curriculum should be balanced, not exclusive. My teaching partner and I decided to teach about all five major world religions and several secular and cultural holidays. They included: Judaism, Christianity, Buddhism, Hinduism, and Islam. We spent a full week on each one and included Kwanzaa and Santa Claus. We focused on the light source for each of the religions—the menorah, Advent wreath, butter lamp, diyas, fanous, kinara and Christmas tree. We posted the school board regulation on the inside of our classroom and informed parents about our approach in the weekly newsletter.

At the end of the unit, we held a "Festival of Lights" buffet in the cafeteria for all parents. We had sample treats and drinks representative of each religious holiday. Children wore their "dressy" clothes and learned how to go through a buffet line, one-by-one. This was the culminating activity of our Celebrations Around the World unit.

The gym was transformed.
Lights dimmed, candles set the mood.
Awareness for all.

Janice Strootman

Section II

Hong Kong

This is Hong Kong!

We received the phone call early on a Wednesday morning–a former principal was calling from Hong Kong. He said he knew our son Paul was off to college in a few months, our daughter was already in school in Arizona, and we'd be empty nesting. What did we think about applying to teach in Hong Kong? We looked at each other in disbelief but assured him we'd think it over.

Our son overheard the conversation and was enthusiastic about the idea. "You guys have to apply! That would be amazing!" Over breakfast, we thought of all the reasons we could *not* do it. It seemed too overwhelming to think about. But once we started talking, the obstacles– tending to our house and cabin, our children away at college in opposite ends of the country– fell like dominoes. "Just think of it this way," Paul said, "you're ten hours away instead of three. No big deal." Our daughter was excited for us, too. She promised to come and visit and reminded us– "Grandma Beta and Uncle Gary are here in Arizona with me."

I told my students about our impending move, and wrote about our new adventure in the weekly newsletter. One of my students went home and told her mother, "Guess what, Mommy? Miss Jan is moving to King Kong!"

Memories in these walls—
looking at the empty house,
I knew it was real.

A New Continent

The school where we were to teach—Hong Kong International School— was started in the 1960s by diplomats and CEOs of businesses from around the world. We were told that we'd be teaching children from forty-one countries, and that parents had high expectations, not just for their children, but for the teachers who were employed there. We would end up teaching very few Chinese students.

We were told what furniture to bring to an empty flat waiting for us in Hong Kong. The school paid for door-to-door shipping–an amazing perk!–but just before we left, we received a call that our flat was not finished. We would have to stay a while at the Park Lane Hotel in Causeway Bay, kitty-corner from Victoria Park, an impressive landmark.

When we first arrived, we were overwhelmed by all the people, traffic, and noise. When we ventured outside, we only walked around the perimeter of the hotel, frightened we'd get lost. Thousands of people, carts loaded with goods, cars and motorcycles were smashed together everywhere. You couldn't tell where the sidewalk ended and the street began. Coming from quiet Minnesota to robust and lively Hong Kong was intimidating for us. The smells of street food and hustle and bustle were all so exciting, and we were in awe of everything we saw.

Vehicles honking!
High-pitched screeching voices yelled.
Bodies pressed on me.

On the morning of our fourth day, school staff picked us up and drove us to our flat in a van. They gave us keys to the front gate, introduced us to the security guards who were on duty 24/7, and gave us a key to the building. The first seven floors of the building were school offices and classrooms, an outdoor gymnasium, and pool. Floors eight through fifteen housed staff, and the sixteenth floor was the laundry room. I was able to take an elevator from our flat on the fifteenth floor to my classroom on the fifth floor. It was very convenient, but it made it too easy to stay for hours after school and to go in on weekends.

Our two-bedroom flat was spacious, with a large living and dining area and small kitchen. From our windows we had an amazing view of the mountains, which were covered with evergreens. The flat was located within walking distance of the beach, where in the future we'd spend our weekends, visiting with colleagues and mingling with local citizens.

Views of green mountains.
Piney smells of the forest.
It felt like a dream.

Out and About in Hong Kong

After a Saturday shopping trip to Central in downtown Hong Kong to pick up cord for my Chinese knot-tying class, I didn't have to wait very long for the double decker 6X bus to our home in Repulse Bay, but there were a lot of people already aboard and several of us queued up to get on.

After I jockeyed around for a standing-room-only spot, the bus took off. I thought we would get to Repulse Bay quickly since the bus was full, but the driver stopped at every collection point along the route, allowing more people to board. We were continually pushed, pulled, tugged and yanked toward the back of the bus. I jumped up on the first step leading to the top of the bus to avoid the crush. However, the people who had gone to the top deck ahead of me had no luck finding a seat so down they came, only to find me in the way. There was no going forward, backwards or sideways.

Alas, one of the more prominent parts of my anatomy was at the most two inches away, and at eye level from a fellow traveler. I wasn't wearing the most supportive undergarment so that part of me was visibly keeping time to the rhythm of the road. We traveled for twenty-five minutes in this position. I think the bus driver hit every bump in the road at least twice. I tried not to look at the passenger who was forced to take in this spectacle. He and his wife were quietly speaking Mandarin. Fortunately, she faced the other direction. When we were finally able to move, he smirked at me and said, "Nice to meet you!" I was glad it was my stop.

With burning red cheeks
I pushed my way off the bus.
Take more time dressing!

Social Studies in Hong Kong

When I taught the five major religions in Hong Kong, my colleagues and I invited a rabbi to speak about Hanukkah. He brought a menorah and other items to show the students. One of the little girls in my class sat down on the floor with her classmates and said, "That's me, Miss Jan, that's me!" She saw herself represented in the school curriculum and her smile was as wide as the sky.

I taught in a large room with three other teachers, and classes from other grade levels walked through our room to get to the outside playground. I was putting information about Divali on the bulletin board when a third-grade class walked by. One of the students stopped and stepped out of line. He looked at the bulletin board and asked, "How do you know about Divali?" I told him that I taught my kindergartners about Divali. "I know about Divali!" he said. "I celebrate Divali at my house!" He walked off, muttering, "I can't believe it! I can't believe it! She teaches about Divali!"

Janice Strootman

Respect for others.
We need to feel we belong.
Include everyone.

We're Not in Kansas Anymore

Just before the December holidays, I asked students what they would be doing during their time off from school. One of my students said, "I am going to Bali." Another student piped up: "We went there last year. There is the coolest waterslide at the Marriott Hotel!" Another student said, "We are going to Jakarta to pick up my baby sister! She is being adopted by us!" Another student said, "We are going to Kota Kinabalu in Borneo to look at the monkeys and swim."

Over the river
to Grandmother's house we don't.
Wondrous lands instead!

Janice Strootman

Dripping with Diamonds

In Hong Kong, the main fundraiser for the school was the annual foundation ball. It was held at an exclusive hotel downtown. Parents of children who attended the school held high-level positions in show business, media, government, and finance, and we teachers were invited by them to attend. Denny wore his tailor-made tuxedo from Kowloon. I wore a Chinese-style silver-infused women's black tuxedo with mandarin collar and jeweled toggles. I had purchased it from Marshall's, a discount department store, back in Minnesota.

We were escorted into a ballroom which was decorated from floor to ceiling with real flowers and lavish lace. Our table centerpieces were roses—red, yellow, pink and white. Green and blue silk ribbons dangled from high ceilings and complemented the table settings beautifully. Chinese blue porcelain dishes, gold silverware, tall etched Waterford crystal goblets, and bright red damask napkins greeted us as we were seated at a round table that had places for ten. We were relieved to see three other teaching couples seated at our table, and we immediately started chatting and laughing, looking forward to a fun evening.

Just before the lights dimmed for a greeting by the PTA chairperson, a maître d' escorted an elderly lady to our table. She wore a tiara, huge, dangling diamond earrings, a diamond choker, three diamond necklaces of varying lengths, six diamond bracelets–three on each wrist–and four enormous diamond rings– two on each hand. Her dress sparkled with hand-sewn diamonds on the bodice. She carried a small but ornate diamond encrusted bag in her hands. She was a tiny woman, but the dazzling light that emanated from her hurt my eyes.

All talking stopped at our table as she was seated. We couldn't help but stare at her. She stared back at us over eyeglasses, rimmed with diamonds. She had a hard stare that settled on each of us individually to the point of making us feel uncomfortable. After what seemed like an eternity, she motioned to the maître d' who had taken up residence a few feet away from her. When he leaned in to listen to her, we could clearly hear her say "It appears I have been seated with a bunch of teachers. That is inappropriate!" He pulled out her chair and she rose, turned her back on us, and left the table. We later learned she and her late husband were the owners of the hotel.

Burying our dismay and the slight we had just received, another table mate motioned our maître d' to our table and said, "Please be so kind as to not seat anyone else at our table. We are *good enough* for each other." The maitre'd smirked slightly, bowed and said, "As you wish, sir." We continued to have a wonderfully fun evening enjoying our seven-course dinner, surprised only when the PTA president said, " The best book is…the checkbook! That's what I tell my daughter."

At the end of the evening, the PTA president announced that teachers were "allowed" to take the elegant floral arrangements and the small ornately wrapped gifts that were in the middle of the table. Having no shame, we all took what we wanted and majestically walked out to the taxi stand, where we shared taxis and split fares to homes, also provided by the school.

Dressed up and ready
for a free dinner and fun.
We do have our place.

Different but the Same

September 11 happened just two weeks after the start of our second school year in Hong Kong. We had come home from school and were preparing dinner when Denny's mom called from Minnesota—were we watching what was happening in New York? We turned on the TV. It seemed surreal.

Planes hit the towers.
SKY NEWS was broadcasting live.
People jumped through smoke.

The next day, my students and I continued our lesson on Maslow's Hierarchy of Needs, as well as personal space and safety in the classroom. One student, whose uncle had jumped from one of the Twin Towers said, "My uncle wasn't safe when he was in New York, was he?" I agreed he had not been and asked if he had talked to his mom and dad about what had happened to his uncle. He told me they were too sad to discuss it. I did my best to explain what had happened in New York as it related to our basic needs and safety discussion. I was shocked to realize how connected we are, no matter where we live on the planet. We had flown halfway around the world, and yet, this little boy was directly affected by what had happened in the U.S.

Many people died.
That event affected all.
Can we stop the hate?

Who Am I?

I would often walk down the hill from school to the Repulse Bay Hotel to shop at Wellcome Grocery Store, located on the main floor. The hotel, a famous landmark, was built with a hole in the middle of the complex, which was said to give the dragon room to fly from the mountains to the sea. The hotel had been converted to apartments years before, and housed numerous families whose children attended the school.

One day, I saw a Chinese student of mine with her mom and "helper." Most of the families I taught at the school had hired Filipino women to care for their children and to help maintain their households. My student saw me with my shopping cart and hid behind her mother's skirt. She appeared shocked and whispered loudly to her helper, "There is my teacher! Is she a real person, too?" I couldn't help but laugh. I told her that I was indeed real and lifted up the mangoes and gestured to the fresh bread I was buying.

When shopping, we had to rely on the pictures on canned goods because we couldn't read the words. We were surprised more than once. A can of tomatoes had baby shrimps in it, what I thought was hair shampoo was actually dish soap and a package of cookies was really salty crackers. We quickly learned to adjust our palates and expectations.

Later, I sat on the half-wall outside of the store, as I often did, eating my mango, and enjoying the smell of the South China Sea. I could feel sweat running down my back, and I was tempted to jump in the water, but remembered I had recently seen the undulating movement of a water snake in this spot. I watched the three layers of boat traffic—cargo ships way out in the harbor, ferries and yachts a little closer, junks–Chinese fishing boats made of wood–and sailboats closest to shore, and thought about how lucky I was to be living in Hong Kong.

Junks made out of wood.
We rented them for parties.
We ate fish and rice.

Janice Strootman

Section III

Minsk, Belarus,

Liptovsky Mikulas, Slovakia

Janice Strootman

Marty and Marie and Minsk

Denny and I thought we were done teaching—we had just retired for the second time—but it turns out we had more in store. We met a couple at our condo in Bloomington, Marty and Marie, who had just returned from Yemen after working for QSI (Quality Schools International). Marty was the director of the school there. He encouraged us to apply to teach at one of the QSI schools. We did some research and found that there were openings in Minsk, Belarus for both of us. We had always wanted to live and work in Europe, and here was our opportunity. We applied, interviewed, and were accepted. I taught Reception 1, which meant sixteen four-year-olds, and Denny taught high school social sciences–geography, history, economics, sociology.

Cabin pipes were drained.
Stopped mail and locked condo door.
Here we go again!

The Trolley Bus

Negotiating around Belarus was difficult because few people on the street spoke English. Most of the staff at the school were fluent, and at the very least, understandable. On weekends, when we felt brave enough to venture out on our own, we took the trolley bus (trooley boos) from our apartment to downtown Minsk. Women in Minsk are incredibly beautiful and dress to the nines. I was in awe of how they walked around in 6" high-heeled shoes and boots, even in the winter!

Where did they buy these shoes and boots? Denny and I were exploring downtown and found a side street where we had not ventured. It was full of shoe stores! I told Den I wanted to look in them, which I knew didn't interest him one bit. He showed me where to catch the trolley bus back to our flat, and I left to explore on my own. When it was time for me to go home, I realized I had ventured away from the trolley stop. I was lost.

I looked around and saw a parking lot where a man was loading a stroller in the back of his car. I hurried across the street gesturing wildly to him, trying to mimic a trolley bus. He stood totally silent, and I repeated myself several times and added in some new gestures. After what seemed like forever, I finally stopped, feeling defeated. He calmly looked at me and said, in perfect English, "It looks and sounds like you are looking for the trolley bus. Is that correct?"

My mouth dropped and I stared at him, dumbfounded. "You speak English? Why didn't you say so?"

He smiled at me and said, "It was far too entertaining to watch you act out what you needed. It made my day!"

I felt so embarrassed, I could feel the blood rushing to my face. He told me where to find it, and I slunk back across the street.

Stay around the school
or look for young teenagers.
They can speak English.

Dandelion Love

My lovely, fair-skinned, long blonde-haired aide Olga and I used to sit outside and pick the long-stemmed dandelions. She showed me how to make braided headpieces. The dandelions were huge there, maybe because Chernobyl was nearby. It was like a scene from *The Sound of Music*, where the hills were alive with yellow.

The children sat in a circle, their eyes locked on Olga as she softly spoke instructions. Her calm, loving manner made everyone feel peaceful. Our sixteen four-year-olds were mesmerized by her long, smooth fingers as they delicately wove one stem over the over. A few of the boisterous boys sat next to me, and I held a flower under their chins and chanted:

"Do you like butter?
Come and sit down next to me.
Are you rich and free?"

If I could see yellow reflected on the underside of their chins, they would stand up, twirl around with arms outstretched and say, "Wheeeeee!" If not, they would stand and say, "Not today! It's time to play!" The kids took their flowers and chased their friends all over the playground while the hairpiece braiding continued.

Dandelion love.
We like and dislike them so.
A weed? Too pretty.

Here they Come, Miss Jan! Here they Come!

When it rained in Minsk, it rained hard. My students found some worms on the playground after a long, three-day rain. I didn't know what kind of worms they were, but thought we could keep them in our classroom and see if they would make compost. We put a few snack scraps in a clear plastic box and mixed them up in potting soil. Orange peels, lettuce, newspaper scraps all went into the mix. The kids were eager to find worms on the sidewalks after a rain. I explained how their tunnels would flood, forcing them to evacuate.

One day, it started to sprinkle and Ian stopped, turned around with his arms outstretched and said, "Watch out, Miss Jan, watch out. Here they come! " I had a puzzled look on my face and he said, "The worms, Miss Jan, the worms!" I guess I forgot to tell them the worms wouldn't rush out instantly.

Enthusiasm!
The worms lost their homes to rain.
They had not drowned.

Janice Strootman

You Counted?

"I am going to count backwards from three, everyone! When I get to zero, I need you to be…" I put three fingers in the air and made a big deal of saying each number in a no-nonsense voice. I found this to be an effective behavior management tool.

My four-year-old students were a rambunctious group. I had two little boys, Diego and Boris, who tested this sixty-five-year-old teacher's patience regularly. They were the only students who spoke English, but their behavior was difficult to manage. One day, before dismissal, Diego and Boris were wrestling and fighting on the carpet. The rest of the class were already seated cross-legged in front of me. I sat Diego down on the outside of my left leg and Boris on the outside of my right leg. I said to them, "You guys are something else! I think I have asked you at least 5, 967 times to please not wrestle!" One of my other students, Ivan, looked at me in shock and said, "You counted?"

It is possible
to be socially astute
at four years of age.

Janice Strootman

Mine is Bigger than Yours

These same two little boys, Diego with his long, curly, dark hair, and short, blonde-haired Boris, were in line outside the lunchroom waiting for a table. I was standing around the corner from them when I heard one say, "Mine is bigger than yours!" The other one said, "No, mine is bigger!" I quickly rounded the corner expecting to see their bare bottoms. Instead, I found them waving their index fingers in the air, sporting the biggest boogers I had ever seen.

Our chef had made stew
that looked a lot like boogers.
No longer hungry.

Moving Up

Having returned from Minsk and having retired for the third time, back home in Minnesota, we enjoyed a glass of wine with our cabin neighbors, pleased to have put our cabins to bed after another season. Bill and Kathy had been teaching English in Slovakia and wondered if we would be interested. We loved teaching in Belarus and wanted to learn more about, and live in Europe, so we spent fall, winter and spring filling out a lot of forms, going through interviews, and finally—packing.

I sat with six suitcases on the curb outside our condo, waiting for our taxi. Their contents would have to see us through a full year of living in Slovakia. We knew a flat was provided for us, but we did not know about furnishings. We also knew the seasons were similar to Minnesota, so we needed to pack boots, warm jackets, hats, and gloves. That took one box. Another was full of school supplies to decorate a classroom. I also packed ESL (English as a Second Language) materials that I had used while teaching adults in St. Francis, seven miles from our cabin. The remaining boxes contained clothing, electronics, and a few kitchen and personal items. The taxi driver was surprised we weren't taking more luggage for a whole year. We told him we had done this twice before and at this point we were getting pretty good at it!

We were assigned a school in Liptovsky Mikulas, in the middle of Slovakia. We would teach English to high school students. We were placed there because we had experience living and teaching overseas—we knew we would have to learn on our own how to maneuver without a lot of support. Bratislava, the capital, was a three-hour train ride away. The scenery on the way to Mikulas was full of steaming hot springs, white-capped mountains, miles and miles of solid green pine forests and charming red-roofed houses bordered by stone fences.

We noticed on our train from Bratislava to Mikulas that the conductor didn't stop for very long. We wondered how in the world we could get our six pieces of luggage off the train in just a few seconds.

When our stop approached, we nervously arranged our bags close to the train steps. We thought we might push them off and jump down after them. The train stopped, and we did just that! Thankfully, there was a muscled young man waiting on the sidewalk, and he came to our aid. If he hadn't, we would never have gotten our stuff clear of the tracks.

The two principals of the schools, both elementary and high school, were at the station. When they saw us, they ran toward us, apologizing for not being at the right spot to help and introduced themselves as Patricia and Sasha. Patricia told us to call her Patka. I know I looked and felt disheveled, because my gray hair was blowing all over the front of my face, and I grimaced jumping off the train. At sixty-eight and sporting two total knee replacements, that wasn't the easiest thing to do!

Patka drove to our flat, a quick block from the station. The car stopped in front of a lime green concrete box, seven stories high with tiny balconies. Home! Patka told us the apartment belonged to a friend of her mother's, and she rented it out for extra income to lectors teaching at the school. At the front door, we received keys to the building and to our flat. Inside, there was a grated elevator door that we opened. Only two of us and one box fit inside at a time. We closed the grated door, then the inside solid metal door, and hit the button that said "5". After several jerks and starts, we were on our way.

Patka and I went up first. When the door of the flat opened, I immediately smelled "grandmother." I inhaled old wood and lingering sweet scents emanating from empty, colorful perfume bottles displayed on a shelf inside the door. Intricate hand crocheted doilies hung from the edges of bookshelves. I instantly fell in love with it. Tension fell from my shoulders, and I stood transfixed, taking it all in.

I must have had a big smile on my face because Patka said, "You like it, then?" I nodded and noticed the bathroom also just inside the door. It had a clawfoot bathtub! Now I knew I was in heaven! There was a shower attachment on the wall, toilet with tank above it sporting a pull chain, sink and mirror. Perfect! Next was the kitchen. The view from the window was the hillside with a trail leading to the top. No buildings, just lush, tall, grasses waving in the wind.

There was a spacious living room with built-in wardrobes and cupboards along the wall between the entrances to two bedrooms. The wood was honey-colored, a big picture window looked across another empty field, and the school was visible on the other side. It was thrilling to see that we could easily walk to school. When we stood on the tiny balcony, we could see the landmark mountain of Slovakia, called Krivan.

Screeching train cars braked.
Whistles announced arrivals.
Students jumped down steps.

Treading on Quicksand

When teaching started, I had three particularly challenging classes. The students did not appear interested in learning English. Talking out of turn, writing on desks, eye-rolling, and use of cell phones all greeted me the first day.

I knew I had to get the respect of the students if I wanted to have a successful school year. I quickly spotted the ringleaders and was prepared for them the second day. I found a cardboard box and set it on the corner of my desk. I told students their cellphones needed to go in the box before they sat down in their new assigned seats. I told them if they could refrain from talking when someone else was talking, the next day they could sit where they wanted. A couple students made it a point to talk over me and a few other students, but they didn't do it the next week. Their peers had been affected, too, and told them to be quiet so they could sit where they wanted. When students wrote on their desks, I kept them after dismissal to clean off the writing. They didn't appreciate being kept after class so that behavior stopped. I stood close to unruly students as I was talking but would not make eye contact. They didn't like that, either. I was very matter of fact about what I needed in my classroom.

The kids liked to have their pictures taken, so I photographed them regularly and posted the pictures on the bulletin board outside the classrooms. I respected all of my students and made it a point to learn all their names and take an interest in them. Natasha warmed when I complimented her amazing drawings of faces, and Ari bonded with me over his beloved motorcycle when I told him I used to have one too. When the miscreants realized that, they stopped misbehaving and became beloved students. I enjoyed the conversations I had with them. We talked about class cheating, birth control, conflicts with family members, smoking, party life, and plans after graduation. In some ways, it was different to teach at high school level, but in other ways, it was a lot like kindergarten.

Intense teenagers.
I learned more than the students—
rollercoaster ride!

What Should I Teach?

We had textbooks for teaching English to high school students, but I found them difficult to use when it came to teaching students outside of the US—all the examples were from places like California. When we prepared for our first week, I asked Denny what he planned to teach his sophomore classes. He had taught social science in Minnesota and geography was his passion. He scrunched up his face, looked over at me and said, "I think I'll teach about continental drift and ocean tides."

Hand on chin, I stared into space and asked myself what I was going to teach these kids. What did I know that would benefit them? I knew phonics, I knew songs, poems, jingles, how to teach reading. These students needed lessons on pronunciation, so I researched poems appropriate for junior high and high school students. I found a British poet Ken Nesbitt, whose work I thought students would love.

When classes began, I walked up and down the aisles, clapping out rhythms and had them repeat.

They looked at each other out of the corners of their eyes and covered their mouths with their hands and smirked. Who was this old lady acting goofy in their class? It took a couple of weeks before the kids loosened up but they did. Their use of "v" and "w" improved greatly as did their diction and syntax. Plus, we all had fun and laughed a lot. By the end of September, I hit my stride and realized I could teach these kids.

In June, all my students could recite the poem *Stopping by Woods on a Snowy Evening* by Robert Frost, from memory. Today, they will quote parts of it in their emails to me. The students told me they wanted to sound like my husband and me when they talked. They were attentive and fully participated in activities. Whew! At the beginning, I wasn't sure I would figure out what to do.

Trust your gut feelings
in unknown situations.
They are quite useful.

Maybe Not!

Twice a week I went over to the elementary school adjacent to the high school to work with fifth and sixth-grade students. I used some of the same jingles, poems, and songs I used with older students and incorporated a lot more movement. This worked well because eleven-to thirteen-year-olds need to move!

I made out a seating chart for them because there were two rambunctious boys and several talkative girls in the classes. I worked with these students right after lunch and before recess, so I had to tap dance as fast as I could to hold their attention. They were sweet kids but very active. I held on to the belief that their English was improving in spite of their inattention.

At the end of the year, the kids gave me going away presents. One little girl gave me a card I could tell she had spent a lot of time carefully drawing and coloring. On the front, she had written "Goodbye, Mrs. Strootman, you is a good teacher!"

I smiled at her and thought, 'maybe not!' I still have that card. I framed it and put it on my display shelf.

Learning can be hard.
To teach is humbling.
She melted my heart.

Sadness to Joy

One day, when I walked into my first hour class, I noticed the quiet. No one was talking and there were candles lit around the room and two sitting on Bianca's chair. I stopped in my tracks and looked around. What had happened? I wrote the poem below to capture the scene.

Bianca

She was here yesterday,
eyes laughing at life.
Her chair is empty today
with candles alight.
Snowflakes she made
hung, taped to the ledge.
Shoes sit empty
under her desk.
We sit in a circle,
and talk about her—
things she liked, said and did.
Her stories emerge.
We hold hands and pray.
I stand by each one,
I see their distress
and feel so numb.
I hug each one
and feel their pain
over and over,
again and again.
A car accident
took her, not her mother.

Janice Strootman

She left her sister, her father,
and brother.
What else should I say?
Hands joined in care.
We sit in silence,
Together, we're here.

After that class period, I had three flights of stairs to climb, and during the climb, I had to figure out how I was going to approach my next class. They had told me the week before that I was going to learn a Christmas song in Slovak and that we were having a dance party, complete with treats.

Students on third floor didn't know students on first floor, so they were unaware of Bianca's death. I stopped outside their classroom door, took a deep breath and opened the door. A blast of music, young people talking and laughing and dancing assaulted my eyes and ears.

"Mrs. Strootman, Mrs. Strootman come and join the party! We've been waiting for you!" One student came up to me, holding out a tin of cookies and said, "My grandmother made these just for you!" I forced my face to smile and resolutely walked over to my desk. My insides were numb. I wanted to sit and cry for hours, but I stuffed my emotions deep down inside and walked to the back of the room to join the party.

I opened the box.
Sprinkled sugar cookies blurred.
They thought I felt joy.

Janice Strootman

EPILOGUE:

BWCA—Unwinding the Year

Boundary Waters Canoe Area, magic words to me. I started going there with a church-sponsored group and fell in love. Nature and women friends, ahhh. The BWCA trip followed each of my years in a Minnesota kindergarten classroom, and I looked forward to the relaxation and break in routine.

The second full day of the trip, after we had set up camp and performed the necessary tasks needed for a comfortable stay in the woods, I would swim out to a rock by myself. I'd find a nice flat one cushioned by dropped pine needles, settle in and listen.

Loons chortle welcome,
smells of pungent pines waft past–
thoughts melt into clouds.

I reflected on the past school year. I started with June and worked my way backwards until I reached August. I unwound each month in my mind. What skill level were my students during each month of the year? What did we study? What centers did I set up for children to explore? By the time I reached August, my mind was ready to begin a new school year. I wanted to unwrap each month like layers of a corn husk, soon to bare the beginning kernels of learning.

And so I did.

Janice Strootman

Janice Strootman

Made in the USA
Middletown, DE
25 October 2022

13411568R00068